Gillian Bickley
Over the Years
Selected Collected Poems 1972-2015
Chosen by Verner Bickley
Proverse Hong Kong
2017

The poems collected in Gillian Bickley's **Over The Years** have been selected from her five previously published collections, four of which received publication grants from Hong Kong Arts Development Council. All except one have accompanying audio recordings of all poems read by herself.

Dr Gillian Bickley (née Workman) was born and educated in the United Kingdom. She has held full-time academic positions teaching Literature in English at the University of Lagos (Nigeria), the University of Hong Kong, the University of Auckland (New Zealand) and retired as Associate Professor in the Department of English Language and Literature from Hong Kong Baptist University after twenty-two years of service there. She has lived and worked in Hong Kong since 1970 except for three years when living and teaching in New Zealand.

She is the biographer of the founder of Hong Kong Government Education, Dr Frederick Stewart, first principal of what is now known as Queen's College, and of the first bishop of Victoria, Dr George Smith.

Her poetry collections are: *For the Record* (2003), *Moving House* (2005), *Sightings* (2007), *China Suite* (2009) and *Perceptions* (2012). The first two of these collections have been translated and published in Chinese; individual poems have been translated into several languages, including Arabic, Chinese, Czech and Turkish and anthologised in Hong Kong, the Philippines, Romania and the United Kingdom. In July 2014, at the 18th International Festival, "Curtea de Argeş Poetry Nights", held in Romania, she was awarded the "Grand Prix Orient-Occident Des Arts" by the Festival Board. In 2016, a selection from her published poems was published in Romania in a bilingual English/Romanian edition, "Poems / Poeme", by Editura Academiei Internaţionale Orient-Occident. In 2017, a similar selection from her collected published poems was translated into Italian by Luisa Ternau, as *Avvistamenti, pensieri, e sentimenti*. Bickley is one of the Hong Kong poets discussed in Agnes S. L. Lam's study, *Becoming poets: The Asian English Experience*.

From time to time she teaches creative writing at the School of Professional and Continuing Education, University of Hong Kong.

Over the Years
Selected Collected Poems
1972-2015

Gillian Bickley

Chosen by Verner Bickley

Proverse Hong Kong

Over the Years
Selected Collected Poems 1972-2015
By Gillian Bickley
Chosen by Verner Bickley.
1st edition published in paperback in Hong Kong
by Proverse Hong Kong, 27 April 2017.
Copyright © Gillian Bickley, 27 April 2017.
ISBN: 978-988-8228-75-1

Distribution (Hong Kong and worldwide):
The Chinese University Press of Hong Kong,
The Chinese University of Hong Kong,
Shatin, New Territories, Hong Kong SAR.
Email: cup-bus@cuhk.edu.hk; Web: www.chineseupress.com

Distribution (United Kingdom):
Christine Penney, Stratford-upon-Avon, Warwickshire CV37 6DN, UK.
Email: chrisp@proversepublishing.com

Alternate edition available from: https://createspace.com/6888674

Distribution and other enquiries to:
Proverse Hong Kong, P.O. Box 259, Tung Chung Post Office,
Tung Chung, Lantau Island, NT, Hong Kong SAR, China.
Email: proverse@netvigator.com; Web: www.proversepublishing.com

The right of Gillian Bickley to be identified
as the author of this work
has been asserted by her in accordance with
the Copyright, Designs and Patents Act 1988.

Cover photograph by and © Proverse Hong Kong.
Cover design by Pin-Key Design. Page design by Proverse Hong Kong.

All rights reserved. No part of this publication may be reproduced, stored in a retrieval system, or transmitted, in any form or by any means, electronic, mechanical, photocopying, recording or otherwise, without the prior written permission of the publisher or publisher and author. The book is sold subject to the condition that it shall not, by way of trade or otherwise, be lent, re-sold, hired out or otherwise circulated without the author's prior written consent in any form of binding or cover other than that in which it is published and without a similar condition including this condition being imposed on the subsequent owner or purchaser. Please contact Proverse Hong Kong (acting as agent for the author) in writing, to request any and all permissions (including but not restricted to republishing, inclusion in anthologies, translation, reading, performance and use as set pieces in examinations and festivals).

British Library Cataloguing in Publication Data
A catalogue record is available from the British Library

Dedicated to Verner Bickley

and the many seen, known or thought about
over the years

Prior Publication Acknowledgements

'Ching Ming Festival' was first published in a Hong Kong Baptist University English Society publication.

'The Flute-player: Sweet and Low', was first published in the English Speaking Union (Hong Kong) on-line Newsletter, 2007.

'Seen in Shanghai' was first published in *IMPRINT 2009: the Annual Anthology of the Women in Publishing Society*, Hong Kong.

All have previously been published (some in earlier versions) in one of the following collections of Gillian Bickley's poetry:

For the Record (2003),
Moving House (2005),
Sightings (2007),
China Suite (2009),
Perceptions (2012).

Over the Years
Selected Collected Poems 1972-2015
Table of Contents

Prior Publication Acknowledgements	6
From "For The Record"	
For the Record	11
Survival	12
The Creator Commands His Own Creation	13
Second Thoughts	16
Moon-Shine	18
Ching Ming Festival, April the Fifth, 1991	21
Memories Of School: Admiration	25
An Intense Desire to be Oneself	26
From "Moving House"	
Past Present	29
Christmas Letters from Afar	30
Fortune Teller	31
Scene in the Street: Handing Gloves	33
Progressive Movement	34
Conferees	35
(Em-) Brace (-let)	36
Change with Constancy	37
A Pure Devotion	39
What I Wanted to Say	40
From "Sightings"	
Super-ego	42
Take up your Bed and Walk!	43
Politically Correct?	44
Parish Priest	45
Walking Stick	46
Transit Lounge	47
White Flags	48

Fragile Symbols	49
Her Choice	50
Aperçus: Encountered on a Walk around the Peak	54
The Watcher Watched	58

From "China Suite"

Wish you were here in Hong Kong	59
Seen in Shanghai	62
Gangways	64
Fisherwoman II: She Loved the Sea.	65
Applause *or* A Simply Ambiguous Life	67
Communicable Smile	69
The Flute-player: Sweet and Low	70
Penates	71
Word-diggers	73
Caring Professionals	76
Pumpkin Man	78

From "Perceptions"

Added Value	79
Change, Please!	83
The Aim of Life	86
International Intimacies	90
Cats	92
Embodiment	96
Choices	97
Eden Marriage Registry	98
I Touched the Wall	100
Water	103

Editor's Choice	105
Message from Dumitru M. Ion	111
Notes	113

OVER THE YEARS

For the Record

On a showing of slides of images of old Hong Kong kept in the Hong Kong Public Records Office, then newly established.

We sit in a darkened room,
gazing at the bright screen, where
images of old Hong Kong appear.

An eerie silence drains the scenes:
Few people; little life that moves.
Only buildings, low, with colonnades; huge trees;
the Peak, now lush and verdant, bare like a moonscape.

It is cosy in the room, manageable, known;
Getting the history books in order
Before new possessors come.

People came and went about their business,
crossing the lenses of old cameras;
but they—intent on things that stayed
more permanently—
ignored them, made no record.

Will the Chinese cameras,
moving in terms of centuries, not hours,
notice us
at all?

1972

Survival

Thank you trees for being there, for staying
when many of the friends you knew—
birds and butterflies—have gone;
for flourishing, even; growing old
here, where concrete buildings
are constantly knocked down.

How brave you are to survive
in a place where the air is foul
and the noise unnatural;
you, who should normally expect
to stabilise your roots
in humid humming forests,
alive with the smells
of animal and vegetable life
(not the smells of mineral death, as here).

It is good to look down a street
and, amazed, to see you there,
solid and green and cool, uncompromised
by the advertising posters on your boles;

a promise

that, since there was a past,
there may quite possibly be a future too.

1982

The Creator Commands His Own Creation

On the first performance by the Cleveland Orchestra at the Tenth Hong Kong Arts Festival.

Lorin Maazel, what does it feel like
as you walk onto the stage of Hong Kong
jet-lagged

all those notes in your head
all those sounds and shapes
rhythms and moods...

Are you aware of the audience,
much aware of the souls
in the orchestra?

Or are you simply
immanent
with the music

heavy with the music
that you need no score
to conduct?

Aware of the crowded platform
around you
only as the plastic chaos
out of which
you will command
creation?

You <u>are</u> imperative.
Impatient to deliver
you command immediate labour.

Joyously, with the discipline
of plenitude,
the orchestra
midwives
at your direction.

Many men
must envy you
your potency, your skill.

Upright and lithe,
single-minded, determined,
energetic and absorbed,
instructions issue from the whole of you.

Though the unsmiling face
is even grim,
your body lilts and insists,
creates by its movements
the mellow beauty
and the urgent pattern
of other men's work,
making it yours.

And then we understand.

It is not you who creates the music
but the music that creates you.

All this magnificent sound,
intelligent and moving,
exists
to create at its centre
you.

Though you command it,
it creates you.

All present wonder at this birth.
For now you smile, relax.
You enter into approving relationships with
the first violin and 'cello.

The music has recreated you.

In Hong Kong too, your life is given to you.

1982

Second Thoughts

A week ago, I gave up possessions—
not the ones I have (except the useless ones)—
but the ones I don't have yet.

I cannot spare my life to care for them.
In any case I need the money.
But now I find the loophole I have left myself
is enormous.
I haven't defined the term at all.

What about tools and investments?
I must still need those?

And how many things can be defined this way?
Cars and typewriters,
answer-phones and home-computers
are surely tools;
while oriental carpets,
prints of Hiroshige and Thomas Allom,
must be both:
tools to impress potential clients,
investments against an inflationary future.

And then, self-care.

It's all very well not buying things
that need *me* to care for *them*.
But what about things that care for *me*?
Curling-tongs and hair-dryers, skin-cream and perfume,
an orthopoedic mattress and a suitable chair:
objects that care for my state of mind —
the very possessions I have given up.

I am disappointed to find
my honest intentions
undermined
by experience of filling in tax returns
and the habit of cajoling bureaucrats.

I do not know how to proceed.

1982

Moon-Shine

In this city of multi-storeys,
I rarely look up to the sky.
"It doesn't have enough sky,"
I say to people
who ask me
What Hong Kong
Is Like;

by which I mean,
there is too much here that impedes
our vision of the light.

There aren't even many stars.

For even away from the high-rises,
out at the Village,
where bedroom windows may outlook
at the water, at quiet islands,
even here, the unseen effluvia
of all our human lives and living
obscure the distant light of stars.

This is why the city lights have such compulsion for us.
Theirs is the only nightly twinkling
we can be sure to see.
Sometimes even these are lessened
when oil is short,
and conservation wins a little point.

Man obviously has such a need for twinkling—
to embrace the pure truth
that even after death
calm influence and disembodied
beauty
can
make warm the hearts of living men
comfort and uplift them to love of an
untouchable ideal.

But here in Hong Kong, there is nothing to look *up* to.
And so we climb the Peak and look *down*
at the city lights.

Our pleasure is in neon lights
that soon burn out,
proclaiming the busy-ness of materiality,
the purchasable pleasures of a *daily* life...
things to buy and use and throw away:
flesh, food and raiments.

Once a year, the Chinese climb high places
for a different purpose:
to admire the Moon.

With them they carry lanterns
representing the Moon
by candles and bright paper that can tear and burn.

This morning I looked up.

I saw—between a corridor of buildings—
the full moon
white and alien
cloud-coloured white
with the dark shapes of mountains, deserts, plains.

"Look at the Moon!" I say, surprised, pleased.
The other early riser cannot comprehend this,
this unexpected message.
She clearly thinks, "This is some strange English idiom
not learnt by those who left school after Secondary Five."

She hurries on, down into the subway, where
no light of stars will ever reach.

The moon looks out of place, an exotic visitor
downcast by lack of welcome,
bled pale by lack of understanding.

O Moon, persist, draw deep on your resources.
Compel us to regard you. Here.

1980-1982

Ching Ming Festival, April the Fifth, 1991

On 5 April 1991, Ching Ming Festival, a family of five was badly burned after being surrounded by a hill fire while visiting their ancestors' graves near Liu To Village, on the northwest of Tsing Yi Island, where the traditional occupation is boat-building. The Husband and Wife and their three daughters, Shui-kei, aged eleven, Shui-ki, aged ten and Shui-ka, aged three, were all injured. The fire was started by other grave-sweepers around mid-day, and spread quickly to cover an area of fifty hectares. It took ambulance-men forty-five minutes to reach the family, who were trapped half-way up the hill. They were carried by stretcher to the top of the hill, from where a helicopter took them to the British Military Hospital. Their Ancestor speaks.

Here they come again, my family—
my grandson, my grandson's wife, my three
great grand-daughters. It is good to see them.

Although the view is good from here—I can
see the sea, where boats like those I built
pass in and out of sight; I can see the sky
expressing many moods; the sun moving
in ascending then descending arcs as years go by;
rising and setting as the days progress,
reddening then greying; warming benignly,
or—with equal heart—brutishly burning
the dry grass, combustible as tinder.

I can see the fullness of the bright round moon
at the mid-autumn festival,
the moon lady and the moon rabbit.

But I see no lanterns as I used to see;
the little children, proud and happy,
timid or—though rarely—tearful. It is
a long time since my son showed me his lantern
at the festival. These children, never.
Much time has passed.

The view is good: and the comfortable
hill behind holds me embraced, secure. Yet
it is lonely here. It is good to see them.
Shiu-chi running ahead.
Shiu-kei, the eldest—more responsible—
helping her mother carry the oranges.
And Shiu-ka, I see, is talking now.
Ming-yeung, my Grandson, who bears the sucking pig,
begins to show his years. In not too long
a time, perhaps, he joins my Son, his Father,
lying apart from here; who also sees
the sea, the stars, the sky;
protected by the warm enclosing earth.

But now they talk to me; they share with me
some parts of worldly life; they eat with me
again. The smell of incense and the family
warmth return my thoughts to men.

Beyond us, lower down the hill, neighbours' families
visit their ancestors, in greater numbers
than in previous years, lighting the fragrant joss-sticks.

**

I do not want to feel this heat;
I do not want to listen to it roar,
I do not want to see this light, this burning brightness
that encircles us, too quickly coming near.
I do not care to see the childrens' fear,
my Grandson's helplessness; the panic in their eyes.
I do not like to see their pain, to hear their screams,
to smell their burning flesh.
Running up the hill, passing through the fire,
strangers in heavy clothing come, disciplined, daring the
flames.
They raise my family skilfully, with careful speed,
dressing their burns with routine, but shocked, care.
Climbing more heavily to the as yet unlit peak,
they bear them all away.

The last I see of them,
Ming-yeung, my Grandson,
Wai-yin, his wife, Shui-chi, Shui-kei, Shui-ka,
my three great-grand-daughters,
they are lifted into the sky.

Near me, the burning grass catches, crackles
and flares. Advancing swiftly, it consumes
the suckling pig, bursting the oranges,
blackening the stone that records my name.

Rushing onwards, the fiery wall is challenged
by brave men, resists, advances, falls back,

and ultimately dies.

***

I and my neighbours,
we did not ask this human sacrifice.

Once a year only, we see our family
and we know their life; turning our thoughts back
to their human world;
Then, repossessing a usual calmness of mind,
renewing awareness of hills and sea,
conscious of our place in their existence,
we resume our sentient peace.

The view is good: and the comfortable
hill behind holds me embraced, secure.

Next year, come Ching Ming Festival again,
will there be a family to visit me,
to sustain my memories of earlier,
human, life?

From now on, and for ever,
will it be lonelier here?

1991

Memories Of School: Admiration

When my teacher retired,
she gave a speech at the Old Girls' tea;
quite a long speech,
which she had carefully prepared.

One of the things she said was,
how much pleasure we girls had given her.

Not only the clever girls, she said,
though there were those:
idealists, rebels, revolutionaries,
poets and rational minds;

But beautiful girls with long fingers
and curved necks,
gazing out of the window
with vacant minds;
whom she hesitated to rebuke,
breaking the charming pose.

I thought it wonderful
and wrote her an admiring letter,

to which she tactfully replied,
saying that, sometimes,
we thought more highly of people
than they deserved.

March 2000

An Intense Desire to be Oneself

A few years ago,
a millipede tickled
over
my bare shoulder
in bed
and then marched onto you,

who resisted and touched it
and it
bit you

—"quite painful", you said—
and we spent the rest of the night
in anxious alarm

and the next night,
not finding the creature.

So quite naturally,
when it turned up
in my bath,
I was pleased

and determined
to remove the cause
of our ridiculous and so far
helpless
fear.

But that multi-footed, inch-long,
personality
was equally
determined.
It would not
be hosed down the plug-hole
or drowned
or battered
to death.

And even when,
disgusted with myself,
I cut it in half (not easy to do)
with my nail-scissors,
it still manifested
an intense desire to be itself.

***

The six men in this ward do the same.
They refuse to surrender their wills, their differences.
They refuse to dissolve their sugar or salt
in the cleansing water of this hospital's routine.

They resist
—for a longish
and heroic
while—
a giant's attempt
to destroy <u>them</u>
by all means,

Showing they do not
want
to become
a drop
in the infinite ocean
or to rejoin their source, the sea.

The Christian
assertion
that
the personality
survives
after death
is proved
by this
to be pure observation
with no absolute need
for a certain faith
at all.

October 2001; revised 2017.

Past Present[1]

We miss the past because we came from there:
people and scenes and places, and ways of doing things:

old women, mumping their lips in the sun;
old men, eating their breakfasts
outside a Museum of Heritage,
in any country;
university students, cherishing
school friends, from primary and secondary days.

And I, do I miss the past, too?

Not yet, not yet.

I embrace the present,
in embracing you.

But I surely know,
the past is where we also come from;
and where we're going, too.

March 2004

Christmas Letters from Afar

What was it that Virgil said?

"Like falling autumn leaves..."?

The ghosts of dead souls
pressed close around Æneas,
their visitor,
drawing life from his sacrifice of blood,
as he visited the dark depths of the past;
seeking one soul,
asking it to speak to him.

And here they come, fluttering through the mailbox:—
souls from our pasts, briefly warmed by unselfish thoughts
of us (and others),
stirring us also with new insights,
as we remember them,
think of them,
briefly visit
their present lives,
through our contemplation
of them and theirs;

remembering our lives,
when they were with us
always.

Noted 2003; completed 2004.

Æneas's visit to the Underworld is narrated in Book VI of Virgil's Æneid.

Fortune Teller

Many years ago,
I visited the Temple at Tai Wai;
crossing a small bridge over an open drain;
and viewing, but not turning,
the windmill that gives good luck.

The old wooden temple is still there,
but inaccessible;
hidden behind a new temple, built some yards away:
a taller, grand stone edifice,
with high surrounding walls
and daily flocks of tourists, following flags.

Outside are rows of fortune-tellers' booths.

At one sits a woman,
fairly young, shrewd and sensible,
but also business-like.

Student ambassadors
volunteer to interpret,
as your beautiful granddaughter
seeks advice, on family and studies.

"Ten dollars a question,"
the fortune-teller says.
The girl's three questions become two.

"You're very sure of yourself,"
the pronouncement comes.
"Think of things sometimes from others' points of view;
"but spare some money for yourself sometimes."

A clever woman! The hint
that thirty dollars is not too much
to pay for her advice. The flattery.
But also, the good advice.

Counsel which,
from others, was ignored;
from her, was wondered at,
accepted,
taken aboard.

Not a bad place to take
your adolescent sons and daughters,
when they
won't listen to you!

March 2004

Scene in the Street: Handing Gloves

Buying from a hawker,
I carelessly dropped my gloves and walked away.

Out of the blue, a French woman
tapped my shoulder,
following me
up the escalator,
to join the Deli France queue.

"Two," she said.
"Usually it's one,"
handing them over,
delphically,
but also delicately.

And that was all she said.

Noted c2002; completed 2004.

Progressive Movement

The old man leant into the breeze,
jogging in very slow motion
the other side of the railway track,
and the man-made hill the other side of him.

And it reminded me, so many
years ago, a pillion passenger on a
Kawasaki bike, in New Zealand,
crossing a wide, sunny, windy plain,
leading to a place called "Bull",
I burst out laughing, when,
as it seemed to me,
the power of the bike
and the opposing
force of the pretty strong wind
were so justly balanced,
that I felt we would be perpetually there,
seeking to cross the golden, hot plain,
but constantly held back,
suspended for ever,
between two equal powers.

And I thought also of Alice,
and the Red Queen's precept, that,
in some circumstances, it takes
a great deal of running,
even to stay in one place.

13 April 2004

Conferees

They tumble down the steps...
stout puppies, eager for their food.

Were they as eager as this,
for the mental sustenance
their conference promised them?

Or did the glossy brochure,
the call for papers,
the abstracts of so many words,
and the emailed proposal
lead them only to this?

A chance to chat, to shine,
make new friends, forget close foes;
a free three-course hurried lunch,
and a little variety in the daily grind?

March 2004

(Em-) Brace (-let)

Sturdy little boy at the bus-stop,
wearing thick, clean, pure cotton shirt and shorts,
what woe impels you to scream and cry
and cling to your grannie's thigh
so much and so long?

Is she taking you somewhere you don't want to go?
Are you leaving someone you don't want to leave?

And your grannie, what does she feel,
her thigh embraced by this screaming boy
so much and so long?

Ignoring him doesn't help;
nor shouting at him;
nor pointing a stern finger;
nor swinging him roughly off his feet;
nor sitting him on a rail
and threatening to drop him in a ditch;
nor pretending to take off his shoes.

Will the bus never come, to break their impasse?

Do they still remain at the bus stop, locked
in their deeply felt (expressed or repressed) emotions:
the seemingly obdurate rock of his safety
and the tumultuous waters of the child,
whose bracelet clearly shows
that, any time he almost drowns,
someone, however apparently absent-mindedly,
will lift him out.
23 April 2004

Hong Kong boat people put bracelets on little boys, so that, if they fall into the water, they can easily be lifted out.

Change with Constancy

In the reclamation of land for the construction of the new (Chek Lap Kok) Hong Kong Airport, the island of Chek Lap Kok was joined to the very much bigger Lantau Island. The small temple of the fishermen's goddess, Tin Hau, was taken down. (It has now been reconstructed at new Chek Lap Kok village.) A moving photo of fishermen taking the goddess away appeared in Hong Kong newspapers at the time.

Goddess of the Sea, Tin Hau, speaks.

I have been here for a long long time
facing out to sea, protecting the villagers at Chek Lap Kok.

When the foreigners first came in their big sailing ships,
I was already here.

When the cannon sounded in the Tiger's Mouth,
and the mandarins' power was challenged by the West,
I observed the outcome and the consequence...
more ships that sailed the sea.

And now my villagers are moving me away—
the men that fish my sea,
the women that mourn their men folk's loss—
taking me with them to Tung Chung on Lantau,
where they also go.

I am wearing my silk robe, bordered with pearls, and
my head-dress also is bedecked with pearls.

Before boarding the boat, we take a last look
round the village, saying farewell. The people are
sad to leave. But the big machines that fly
need another place to land; and they want this place of ours.

As for us, the sea (not the sky) is our element. We can find
another place to merge with it, facing its bounties and
banes.

The villagers have changed; but not so much, that they
forget the ways their ancestors have followed.
The clothes they wear are sometimes foreign clothes;
but they eat the dishes that they always ate,
baak choi, choi sum, rice, fish and other vegetables.

The children learn both western knowledge
and our Chinese ways.

But their hearts are mine.

Begun 199[4?]; completed 2004.

A Pure Devotion

It was still there,
the new shrine, that I first saw yesterday.

The gods had nibbled the biscuits in the
thoughtfully opened packet;

but had left the apples, wrapped sweets and
oranges,
for another day.

How ones heart is moved!

Pleased at the thought, that
here is offered thanks for happiness given,

sad in case of a mute plea
for a need to be met,

warmed by the possibility
of an absolutely pure devotion.

December 2003

What I Wanted to Say

After I got the phone call, booked the
flight and was safely seated,
with the seat-belt dutifully round me,
fastened at all times,

I thought about you and what I
should say when I saw you—
already confined on what was certainly
your death-bed.

"The right to know."
This was one of several rights
the web-site listed,
under "hospice" and "pain".
"The right to talk about it," was another.

I remember how I coughed, night after night, one year,
with whooping cough,
and every year afterwards;
and that you were patient and kind.

I remember that you took me out,
one Sunday afternoon, to learn
to ride my new bike. And when I fell off,
said, "Don't tell your Mother!"

I remember that you gave me money
to pay for music lessons,
against my Mother's very clearly-expressed wish.
I remember once, myself an adult,
already away from home some twenty years,
you waited up, for me to come home,
after a mild evening out.

I remember you lent me your car for two weeks,
another year, when I was again home on leave.

I remember and value your praise for two books I wrote.

These were some of the things I wanted to say.

But, how could I tell you kind things,
without making you know what I
knew? Without making explicit
the implicit cause of my being there
with you, at all?

Now, I have one more thing to remember.

You gave me no space to say any of this at all,
protecting me still, as far and as long as
you could; before yourself going away,
for good.

Noted 2001; completed, 2004.

Super-ego

It takes time to search in memory
for stored parts of me,
not used for a long time.

There may be interference:
the questions,
"Is it wise?"
"Why should I?"
and, "Should I?"

Are those parts good, or useful,
or even <u>allowed</u>
by the super-ego I have grown (not quite like a shell;
not quite like a jail)?

But, questioning solved,
the address successfully searched,
I find they are still here.

1982; revised, Summer 2006.

Take up your Bed and Walk!

The frail old man, blue jumpered,
face becoming skull,
crept along,
pushing his wheel chair.
It had a red cushion on the seat,
decorated
with a Chinese character.

If it said, "Long life!"
I hope it also wished him,
"good health!" and at least a
degree of prosperity.

— I always thought that the man
stricken with a palsy
leapt up
and could stride away,
when Jesus said,
"Take up thy bed and walk!"

But perhaps he also
effortfully and slowly
jerked and heaved to his feet,
stood up tremblingly and weak,
and took
long months
really to walk again
as he had walked before.

October 2005

Politically Correct?

I am in a meeting.
Someone has been criticised,
for using the word, "hypocrisy".

He changes his vocabulary:
"Idealism, then," he says.

Goodness, how can he suggest
that hypocrisy and idealism
are <u>the same thing</u>?

But wait...
<u>Does</u> he have a point?

Written c. 1982; edited, 2006.

Parish Priest

We have watched you now for nineteen years;
serious, with your pleasant voice,
asking us questions and answering them,
always the same; asking and answering,
as if you knew we understood few words;
'though—I am sure —you deeply hoped
the Word itself
was something all your congregation deeply knew.

We have watched you growing older,
still serious; and occasionally, in your hands,
saw the odd pleasure of a cigarette;
once or twice noted your brief chat
with doubtless useful parishioners.

Then, some years ago, we found a change.
A younger priest was there,
in the church, which, in your meekness,
probably, you never saw as yours
—except as it was ours, all of ours—too.
But still you sat or stood before us,
sharing the service,
assisting him, who previously assisted you.

And still—no, more and more—your demeanour
teaches us what we should be: selfless, humble,
asserting not your own words,
but the Word made manifest through you.

Ordino, August 2006

Mossèn Roc Pallarés, then retired parish priest of Ordino, Andorrà, passed away on Tuesday, 9 October 2007.

Walking Stick

Walking along the path,
with the stick I gave my Father,
and which he used some years
before he could not stride at all,
let alone pick a footing through
such stony slate and dirt
as on these mountain paths.

I remember...he always took a stick
for country walks;
to indicate some distant view,
to scratch a grateful pig, or lean on,
pausing next to me, his only daughter;
arms full of summer bluebells,
or Easter primroses.

And, as I walk now,
leaning on this stick,
I try to send a message
through its point;
to send him pictures of these homely fields,
the horses' droppings (good for rhubarb),
the startled birds, red campion flowers,
white stitchwort; streams and pools....

Such simple things may be omitted from heaven.

And he would enjoy them still, I know.

Ordino, August 2006

Transit Lounge. (Whiling away the time, waiting for a connecting flight.)

Waiting for hours together in an airport transit lounge,
perspectives change.

Humanity
is reduced
to these half human travelers,
stretched
out
on chairs, carpets and each other;
spirits dampened
by alienating suspension
between
one sphere
and the next.

Life itself is narrowed to these lanes of goods,
this processed food, these selected blandishments
from modern life.

But for me, this relaxed and happy thought arrives
and spreads its calm:

"I could walk with you for ever,
steadily and intimately
progressing,
through the shopping malls of life."

May 2006

White Flags

They tell their message clearly:
white strips of fabric,
lining hillside paths;
the freshly turned earth,
in horseshoe shape,
near to the previously paved
family tomb;
and the red strips,
tied to some living tree.

One being, gone.
And another life,
marked for destruction,
for all to see.

Was the human life slated for death,
equally clearly,
before the axe fell?

How sad for those,
who looked on!
How cruel of those,
who saw,
but did not grieve!

December 2005

Fragile Symbols

Three bright triangular flags
fly bravely, pointing waterwards,
on the margin of the fishermen's island
that we pass, on the way to Tung Chung.

What message do they have for us?
—Survival? Welcome? Veneration? Defiance?—

In quite different cultures,
fragile fabrics carry significances,
stronger than the substance of our individual human lives;
and witness to them longer, too.

Memory calls to mind
heraldic hangings, threadbare
with their ghosts of messages,
in distant, dim English cathedrals,
where instants are lengthened, perpetuated.

The media used are similar;
but the messages, probably, are different.

Each, paradoxically,
communicates only to those,
who know the message already.

Why have the symbols then?
Are we so bad at remembering?

3 November 2005

Her Choice[2]

She was a big woman, tall and stately,
and she always wore white:
white pleated silk skirt, down to her ankles;
white silk stockings;
white leather shoes, with moderately high heels, straps and
    buttons;
a white loose blouse, with long sleeves, flounces, and frills;
and a big white hat, with a half veil,
topped by a big, stuffed, white bird.
Her face was white too, painted with thick powder,
white as flour. She carried a soft silk handbag;
and, in her other hand,
a white parasol in the Edwardian fashion.

We saw her on Sunday afternoons, sometimes;
young girls going to Sunday school.
We stared and looked,
as she measured the city pavement slowly,
undisturbed.

"She lives in such and such a home,"
one of us would say. "But she's alright.
She can come out, whenever she wants.
She was jilted at the altar, ever so long ago,
years and years ago;
and this is what she wore,
as she waited for him, then."

Another story was, that her sweetheart
died in the war—the Great War
(nineteen fourteen-eighteen), that would be.
But always, it was a man,
whom we deemed to be the cause
of her choice for her life.

For, however deeply buried
that choice was, it *was* a
choice, was it not?

Some of us knew her name;
and it seemed strange to me,
that this detached presence
had anything so personal as a name;
that one of us
could have such intimate knowledge
of a personage so august.[3]

Miss What-was-your-name,
what was in your mind,
as you progressed
down the empty Sunday streets,
turning neither right nor left,
always facing straight ahead,
with imperturbable tread?

Stripped of the present,
were they more familiar then?
Did your eye acknowledge only older buildings,
present since your youth?

The Star Hotel, the Angel, and the Crown,[4]
where you may have taken "refreshment";[5]
Pump Street Methodist Church,
which would have frowned if you did;
Grey Friars[6] and the Cathedral (once a monastery church)

—institutions, where surplus males
(accumulated after years of peace,
when man-made selfish folly,
man's clever new inventions
had not yet wiped out
millions of young men,

and by the same slaughter,
stripped their wives and the young girls growing up
of companionship, love, children,
and previously expected purpose)—

White Friars and the Cathedral, then,
where surplus males, in former times,
found a pattern and a style of life,
by which to endure the years;

things you found for yourself,
and which also had, in their own way,
dignity, remarkability, beauty, and a kind of fulfillment.

The Shambles[7] and the Hop Market,[8]
where the grosser needs of food and drink
were copiously—and partly brutally—available;
the Friends' Meeting House,[9]
where your silence would have been nothing unusual;
though its message, some might have thought too violent a
    painful protest;

The Commandery, headquarters, for a time,
in England's bloody civil war;
when puritan—later Protector—Cromwell
and always cavalier King Charles
fought for the life-style they and their people preferred[10]
(as President Mr George born-again-christian Bush
and the Al Quaeda group have each done today);

Foregate Street railway bridge,
bearing the three black pears,
which Worcester—loyal city,
"civis fidelis"[11]—gave to Elizabeth the First,
hundreds of years ago,
when her royal Progress[12] took her there from London:

—an earlier spinster; who found that single state,
and her careful guidance of her English nation State,
callings, worthy of her passionate embrace.—

As for you, late Edwardian dame,
were you there to see, or, like the Queen, to be seen?

Were you refreshing the past,
re-printing old city sights on your mind?
In imagination,
were you walking with your beau,
strolling slowly, enjoying love's young dream,
walking for the sake of it, with no destination
but the heart's fulfillment, which never came?

Or, in your mind's eye, did you see him, waiting for you,
at the end of this long, familiar street?

Were you consciously showing,
with your calm advance,
and focused, undeflected confidence,
his loyal love, your faithful fancy?—
conveying also, but with less intention,
the profound depths, where you had buried
(and for years kept buried) your sharp,
sad knowledge of the cynical way the world had taken,
destroying the dreams of your long-past, decades-old,
        youth?

Seen 1950s; written 2006; revised 2017.

Aperçus: Encountered on a Walk around the Peak

Is it a leaf falling, soundless, brown,
or a butterfly, silently visiting
sites, where nectar was found
last summer?

What a scurry you make
with that long blue tail of yours
whacking the boughs,
cock-pheasant.

Morning-glory,
I did not know
you curled up for the night;
feeling shy,
regretting the recurring
loss of the brighter sky,
and your Father, the sun.

It is difficult to find
the paths we trod last year.
Was it there?
Was it here?

Screechily singing cricket,
rasping like a saw,
or a door that creaks,
are you so small
that you make a big noise
out of fear?

Japanese maple,
with leaves like paper,
wilfully playing games with the wind,
I guess you know
no-one can fine you,
for the litter you make,
just like an under-age child!

Nobody steals
those brooms and those baskets,
trustfully left for tomorrow's work.
—I wonder why?—
Do they fear, the penalty may be
to sweep the Peak for ever?

Jagged epiphyte,
comfortably sitting
in that arched bole,
cushioned smoothly
by round penny-wort;
you chose the very place,
where I would sit, if I were you.

Wildly waggling leaves,
why do you, alone,
move eccentrically?
No animal is digging at your roots,
as I can see.
Do you wish to pull up from the soil,
and so, wildly try, try...
until, by your dancing, you die?

Rook, you sound like a tom-cat
calling a mate. Auw Auw.
And now ererh ererh,
like a cat that has found one.

Black cap, "pink," "pink,"
perky as a pirate;
your grey breast, stained by blood,
why do you fly jerkily away,
when you see that I watch you?

Was I standing so still,
that you thought me a tree
and flew into me,
black butterfly, studded with white?

The mist has come down.
The hills' outlines glow
with the sinking sun.

Time to go home.

Leaves, how can you be
so many shapes and sizes?
Can you still know you are all
close members of one family?

Squirrel, you sat
quite calmly grooming,
until the thump of the runners
was really quite near.
Then you moved smoothly
upward to the tree-tops.
You may be deaf,
but you know that we aren't blind.

Bull-frog, shouting for love in an echoing drain...

The largest group here, on this hill,
seems to be birds:
tramping through the leaves,
as loud as people do.

The waterfall has shrunk.
It sounds like a tap left on,
filling a plastic bucket.

Has a human uprooted you, tree,
that you lie, untidily cumbering the path?
And you in bud too! Ah, cruel!

White flowers! I have finally found
who perfumes the air. It is you!

The islands seem like clouds;
the clouds, like islands.
Twilight magically
twists
how we see
the view.

Trees, be more careful.
If your roots
break up the tarmac
any more,
you will be cut down.

A part of man
partly lives here, too.

Revised, Summer 2006.

The Watcher Watched

An apparently perfectly normal man
held out his arms stiffly like
the wings of a plane,
revolved in a small half-circle,
and went back the way he came.

I stood and watched him
to see if anything else eccentric
would follow, but nothing did.

As I stopped my own eccentric, still, stance,
moved out from the middle of the passageway,
positioned myself to cross the road,
I saw two hard-hatted workers,
sitting on a low wall, resting.
One—all animated—was miming
the first eccentric's airplane movements.
I think he glanced in my direction too,
telling his mate, "That's what
she was watching too, you know"!

Observed May/June 2006; completed, 29 June 2006.

Wish you were here in Hong Kong!

I shall always be disappointed
that my parents came once only to Hong Kong;
rejecting, as it seemed,
all the things I had to share with them, here:

Densely packed mimosa along Siu Wo Road;

The happy wanderer, like Johnny Apple-seed,
with bundle on stick, bouncing down the road
to his public housing estate space
at the end of the day;

Cats he fed tenderly from the back of his truck,
parked at a green garden near a scenic lookout,
and our concern when they disappeared;

Dog excreta in the grass;

The public lavatory with no drainage system,
built by mistake, then reduced to its original intention,
a place for literate dogs to leave their packages;

Noisy buffalo chomping on young trees;

Homing pigeons taking time off, at the side of the path;

Views of the Buddhist Christian study centre, across a deep
    valley;

And in the distance, the entrancing expanse of an encircling
    mountain range;

The gleaming false gold of a butterfly chrysalis;

Make-shift illegal eye-sores of bamboo,
draped with striped polyester sheeting,
with attached bilingual plea:
"This shelter is meant to protect
"early morning walkers
"from the rain.
"Please do not destroy;"

The small rocky stream, with its few mosquitoes whining
overhead;

Junior Police Call's experimental garden,
where enthusiasm waxed and waned;

A commercial garden;

Occasional snakes;

The wooden bench, one plank missing,
which—over a period of years—
we saw gradually reduced to a few, sad, damp, sticks;

Pylons straddling the paths;

Steep sections, where useful handholds going up
became treacherous roots going down;

Music, firecrackers, barking dogs, revving engines
from a village, "down there,"
which we would have loved to visit,
but dared not intrude;

Sweaty fire-fighters marching down the hill,
at the end of a long day's work.
"We have to walk up to the fire," they told us,
"There's no other way to get there;"

The black hill-side, remembrance of some person's
previous carelessness (not to say, "arson");

The middle-class walker with his faithful dog,
who said to us, one day, sadly,
when we asked, "Where's your dog?"
"I am going to tell you something
"you may not want to hear:
"he died;"

The Philippine young man,
sitting on a chunam-plastered slope, at dusk,
facing the valley; not completely alone,
attentive to his bible, singing some hymns aloud,
with his employer's labrador resting nearby.

Hong Kong,
Experienced 1992-2003, edited from notes, 2006.

Seen in Shanghai

In this current of pedestrians,
some separate, some loosely grouped,
they make an eye-catching,
throat-catching couple:

the diffident, self-effacing mother,
with downcast eyes;
finding unbearable our curiosity,
maybe also, fearing our contempt;

son with straight-ahead glance,
proud of his achievements.

She holds his hand,
but I think he thinks
he's holding hers.

A Down's syndrome child
rarely makes thirty birthdays,
so books say. But he looks older.

Of course she loves him.
But her careful love
has multiplied her cares.

Prolonging his affectionate life,
she prolongs the death of personal life
his birth inevitably brought her;
beyond what mothers usually endure.

If—no, when—he leaves her,
will her memories of him
and consciousness she did all well
—her very best and more—
be strong enough, to help her
hatch out of the chrysalis
she shut herself inside;

cocooned from our interest,
cocooning him
from too much knowledge
of himself?

Will her own butterfly unfold its wings then;
at last take to the vivid air?

Shanghai, December 2006.

Gangways

Watching the gangway raised
on to the ferry departing for DB,
peering through the narrowing, closing, gap,
and wondering if I'd catch sight of my husband,
hurrying, to be left behind,
and what I'd feel if I did;

with a catch of the heart,
I thought of those fleeing
some terrible danger,
some desperate—political,
social, or natural—disaster;
seeing their loved ones
left behind.

How infinitely greater their pang of loss;
knowing suddenly
that separation is happening!

What a chasm
separates
the virtual certainty of a very close reunion
from the agony of perceiving possibly final loss.

From such felt experiences of our own,
we glean sharp glimmers of lives
much differently fortunate
but emotionally the same.

Hong Kong, March 2007; revised 2017.

Fisherwoman II: She Loved the Sea

On 7 April 2007, the first sea funerals were held in Hong kong waters for city residents. The daughter of one was interviewed by the "South China Morning Post" and the first line of this poem is what she was reported as saying.

"She loved the sea and often caught fish here."

Yes, I suppose you would. Love it, I mean.
Familiarity can breed love.
And how could one work on the sea,
for hours, days, years, a lifetime,
and not like what one does?

A solitary fisher, perhaps. Thinking of the fish.
Focused on the water, the tides, wind, and other weather.
Perhaps in the calm dwelling on self and family.

A Christian funeral, so a Christian lady.
A Christian family, it seems;
for her tearful daughter spoke of Easter
and God's Easter will.

To be a fisherwoman and a Christian too!
To hear the story of Christ's walk on water!
To know that the first disciples whom Christ called
were fishermen too!
To know how He said to them,
"I will make you fishers of men!"
That, to one of them, Christ said,
"On this rock I will build my church."
To hear the story of the empty nets
miraculously filled.
The story of the loaves and the fishes
and the feeding of the five thousand.

How close she would feel to it all!
And, if she ever went to the town,
to the cathedral there,
saw the tribute to all fishers of fish
glowing in stained glass still,
how cherished she would feel, perhaps;
or, if modest, as I think fisher folk must be,
perhaps too much exposed.

But what would she make of the story
of the Gadarene swine?
—Hearing how devils entered a herd of pigs,
who rushed to the edge of a cliff,
fell over, and drowned in the sea,
did she ever wonder
if there were devils in the flotsam and jetsam
she must frequently have increasingly seen
in the formerly clear deep waters,
always, once, reflecting the sky?

And, her ashes floating as her boat once did,
buoyant on the kindly rocking waves,
sinking down through the depths,
settling among the lobsters she used to catch,

Will she be affronted by harsh coloured plastic,
sharp tins and glass? Or will she know
that the sea will redeem them too? The movement of water
on glass, take away its edge; rust, eat up the tin;
plastic (colonized by moluscs, seaweed and small shoals)
take on real life, not merely dissemble it?

As for those in peril on the sea,
will she reflect that all dangers are now at an end for her?

April 2007

Applause or A Simply Ambiguous Life

We clapped her life, not only her talk,
when it was over. This was my feeling.
Not that her talk didn't
come down the aisles to us
and tell us what we expected.

But her quiet self-possession
(doubtless built on great possessions),
her fairly direct confidences and confidence
(probably built on a life-time's protection)
warmed us to her gentle glow.

But oh yes, as someone said afterwards,
there was probably, "much more to the lady,"
than she was allowed to show.

And indeed, sitting not far from the front,
I heard her disappointed, short-lived protest,
as her interlocutor moved her on,
"But we've left an awful lot out!
"We've said nothing about [an unmentionable subject
now]."

And has that really been her story?
Not allowed to say what she wished.
Not allowed to initiate. Always,
required to respond to what others
had agreed she might be asked to do?
Always constrained by others' views
of what was appropriate for her?

Living in Shanghai as if it was Surbiton,
In Bristol, taught Philosophy, by teachers
old-fashioned even then (these were *her* views);

Marrying the man next door,
whom she met through his parents,
—her childhood patrons—
when he and she were both grown-up:
A fairy-tale in a way.

And then that big house in a posh
neighbourhood, with huge gardens;
near a sandy beach, golf-club and much
quaint local colour. Charity work
of a mild type; a gracious figurehead,
usefully encouraging other wealthy ladies
to shell out themselves and, in turn, to ask
their own less prominent contacts
to donate from their own lesser means.

And so she turns to her family. Perhaps
they will let her say what she thinks.
Her book, ostensibly for her grandchildren,
is, as she says, quite personal:
not for the general public,
where doubtless she places us all.

Why offer it us, then?
Surely, not for the few thousand dollars
you raise by this means
for two small children's charities,
when you control—or maybe only enjoy?—
so much opulence yourself?
Secretly, in your unrebellious
heart of hearts, is this
your way, at long last,
of telling us what you really think?
Or is there still very much more to tell?

Hong Kong, 28 May 2007; revised 2017.

Over the Years: Selected Collected Poems

Communicable Smile

A smile can be like pushing a button;
an action, producing an equivalent reaction.

Walking down the street, one day,
I flashed a bright smile at a janitor,
standing in a doorway, taking the air.

He was surprised,
briefly considered the phenomenon;
then, before I passed out of earshot,
called out, after me,
"Happy Easter!"...

A surprising greeting
in secular Hong Kong,
Buddhist Hong Kong,
Taoist Hong Kong,
but may be more
Christian Hong Kong
than I had realized before.

Hong Kong, Easter (7 April) 2007

The Flute-player: Sweet and Low

The sweetness of his well-played tune
was lovely to hear. Lovely to see
was his seriousness. He sits low
on the ground; here, where we pass
thoughtlessly, wordlessly, ignoringly, by.

But he has worked, sometimes,
as hard for mastery—musical, I mean—
as those we applaud from green plush seats,
comfortable, expensively bought;
calling for encore after encore,
from the high stages,
where not only talent has put them.

His person is unobtrusive. He holds out
no hat or cup for alms. He offers none
of us his story, set out in pleading words,
begging our love.

He gives us what he has, without our asking for it.
Thank him for his gift.

But when you put a coin carefully down,
to nestle where his flute sleeps at night,
thank him with a smile
and some respectful words of praise.

He is an artist too and has his quiet pride.

September 2007

Penates

Approaching our regular holiday home,
I wonder where my underclothes are.

I remember
that small piece of furniture from Hong Kong;
and feel at home again,
in imagination.

And I remember
advice from a women's magazine:
"Always carry with you, when you travel,
something to bond you to where you are travelling to:
a photograph; a picture; a small ornament."

Such good advice.

And then I remember,
this is what the Trojans did too.

Fleeing the Greeks,
"et dona ferentes,"
and their destructive equine gift
(wooden but potent, soon to be in flames)—
which stubborn and misguided priests
saw as offered in religion's name—

they took with them their "Penates,"
their household gods;
something to remind them
where they came from;

to recall their roots, their culture,
their lost dear ones:

seeds for a future
without and beyond them;

in some small way built on them;
in some small way continuing them;

carrying them, too,
into the limitless future

of a new world.

Andorra, July 2007

Word-diggers

Thoughts on research, writing and publishing, partly suggested by the failed intellectual property case that Michael Baigent and Richard Leigh brought, claiming that Dan Brown's novel, "The Da Vinci Code", copied their own book "Holy Blood, Holy Grail" (1982); as discussed in an online article from CNN in London, dated 7 April 2006.

We word-diggers labour like slaves
in the closeted, cold, lonely—often dirty—
depths of the elemental mine of the world's words.

The gold is there. We see its dull shine
and even dig it out from time to time,

shoveling it out

(still firmly embedded
in the hard rock,
where it has lain for years)

onto the wheeled trucks
that carry it to the air.

There, others—high artists—
extract it from the dross, polish it,
mould it to fine objects of high price,
acknowledge us not at all.

But the first work was ours.
We found the gold; it was we,
who separated it from what
was less important,
understanding its potential.

Over the Years: Selected Collected Poems

Others knew its nature
only after we nosed it out,
isolated it, smelt its quality.

We acknowledge their creative work,
of course. But in our hearts,
we feel—considering their place in life—
if roles reversed,
we could do their work;

but partly doubt
they could tolerate ours

given its laborious nature
and the nature of its laboriousness.

As for more popular writers,
they need our gold
to melt, pour and mould
for the people's taste.

It is <u>our</u> gold then, often,
that publishers coin,
passed up to them by agents,
editors and familiar friends,

which in due course returns to them again,
circulating through bookshops,
websites, launch parties and all
the many activities
that produce more funds
for ever much more popular publishing,

swallowing up the gold
we word-slaves find and treasure,

happy to be the pioneers,
the seekers for value and beauty;

but perhaps not entirely happy,
not to be acknowledged
by those who pocket the cash;

not entirely happy that a small percentage,
at least, isn't thrown our way, now and then.

Andorra, Summer 2007.

Caring Professionals

An Anglican clergyman, in Iraq (if I remember correctly), interviewed on British TV after the failed car bomb attacks in London and Glasgow, in early July 2007, said he had a conversation with a Moslem extremist, who said to him, "Those who cure you will kill you!"

"Those who cure you will kill you!"
What would we have made of this,
this occult, dark and threatening forecast,
if someone said it to us?

Certainly, it would puzzle us.

And then, whenever it happened—
days, weeks, months, years later—
that, allegedly, eight medical professionals
failed to kill hundreds
of the British public
whom they were paid to cure,
it would have come back to us
with the staggering comprehension
of hindsight.

***

But now we know what may have happened,
we must concentrate and think,
from what group
the next traitors will be drawn;

consider who will be the next
clever, well-trained, political idiots,
to attack us from within;

and the answer comes so easily,

our priests, of course:
taught to forgive, to love,
to turn the other cheek,
doubtless appalled at war,
death, politics, turmoil,
dishonesty and deceit.

Wouldn't it be easy
for a Moslem imam
—one of those who teaches
packed congregations
to support war, encourage resistance,
and to hate,
unmitigated by any thought
of circumstance or cultural relativity—

Wouldn't it be easy,
for such a man,

to turn a Christian priest
(persuasion immaterial)
to pity the (wrongly-called) Moslem cause,
and pitying, to assist it?

Andorra, Summer 2007; revised 2017.

Pumpkin Man

His skin is thin
as an onion's;
taut as lantern paper.

From his featureless
pumpkin face,
his eyes peer out,
all-seeing.

We fear to meet those eyes,
to find the emotions
behind his horrific, horrifying,
destroyed mask of a face.

He lies there on the walkway,
uncomfortably prone,
cap gesturing for him,
for alms.

But at the end of the day
(one may see, if the timing is right),
he has a home to return to;
stands up,
puts his cap on his head,
walks away.

November 2008

Added Value

The paradoxes in what we were taught!

Injunctions to store up treasure in heaven,
where neither rust nor moth would destroy,
were surely meant to teach us priorities;
Not, to eschew possessions.
Not, to neglect their care and repair.

Inbuilt obsolescence
would otherwise
be just what the Bible ordered—
a continuing lesson
that this world's goods fail us and die.

Advertising even
(in some strange way its twin),
does not hope to make us
covet cars, cookers, or clothes
for themselves,
but for the possibilities
they may facilitate
for spiritual solace, emotional joy.

Does the man exist who values objects
for themselves alone?

That extreme of spiritual poverty—
the miserable miser—
whose love of money has lost sight
of its power to purchase,
presumably loves its power to move his heart?

Over the Years: Selected Collected Poems

The mother who wounds her children's hearts—
shields books, pictures and glass,
carved wood and carpets
from their desire to play—
values the work (the time,
the skill, the patience)
of those who made them;
those who developed technologies,
over variables of time;
those who thought the thoughts
that developing skills have expressed.

She cherishes her own work also:—
the controlled and complicated
easy simplicity which she has made a home.

No wonder, the strength of the work ethic!—
the pealing response,
rung by the added value of Marx!—
since it seems we
naturally
see value
in everything tangible;

either serving the needs of our souls,
or embodying work and creativeness.

Quite naturally, then,
we would value nature and ourselves—
all things that are—
the more; if we thought of them like this:

created by a technologist
of massive range and intellect,
a visionary
with immense power of synthesis,

a being
who took pleasure in the creations of His hands,
expanding His humanity
by their existence,
the possibilities they give
for further work and love.

Should we not
try to embrace this concept?—

extrapolate from our experience of man's works
(what he can do, has done, may do);
from our knowledge of man's many conscious intentions,
seen even in fields and woods,
flowers and breeds of dogs,
milk-yield in cows,
cloud-seeded rainfall,
and babies in test-tubes?

Could we not extrapolate?—

accept the possibility
that conscious intention
made the world and us?

And then—as artifacts—
might we value ourselves the more—
the others we know, the millions we know not,
the beasts and the forests, water and air?—

And if we estimate
the added value of aeons of labour and vision,
factor in
the technological inventiveness and complexity
that made us and the world,

would we not be convinced,
in our own terms,
of what we should value most?

and restore our thoughts, ourselves,
and all things in our power,

to ordered harmony?

Written c. 1982; edited 2006; revised 2007.

Change, Please!

The need for change perceived during a visit to the United States of America.

Is it because I've lived too long in foreign parts,
that I feel it shocking
to find men of European stock in menial jobs,
waiting at tables,
punching tickets on trains?

At first I thought it was.

I've lived so long in places
where they work only
in the professions,
with spectacles, books and suits;
and where their wives (who would quite like
to work in shops, in hairdressers', or hospitals)
can't, because of social pressure
—the same which, in 18th century India
and the 19th century too,
made the English combine, to pay the passage home
of any lesser white—jockey or failed businessman—
who let the side down,
creating (as they felt then) an Achille's heel
in the foot of the mighty Raj—
but there were other reasons too
(language problems,
the need for jobs by the locals,
who lacked expatriate perks).

My assumption had grown to be
that such persons are educated.
So, I think, "What a waste of education
for this man to punch holes in tickets all day long,
telling us, 'Next stop, White Plains:
Change here for local trains!
This train will make White Plains,
One Twenty-Fifth street—One Twenty-Five—
and Grand Central only!'"

But now I know
my feeling is more valuable
than I at first supposed.

In a culture,
whose goals are spiritual unity with the universe,
love of beauty, children, man and woman;

collecting tickets implies no failure;
is irrelevant to the goals of life.

But when career-achievement is the culture's goal,
how lacking, what failures menials are!

Pity the European!

Unless we change his culture,
it is likely that, to save his soul,
he will still want others to be his menials;

and they will accept, because it does not matter
to them to labour.

Their humiliation
exists only in the eyes of some persons from Europe,
who see them,
coloured by different-thinking thoughts.

This produces, most unfortunately,
situations,
making it difficult for the European
to know his own culture's failings.

How can a culture, lived by men—
failures, in his culture's eyes—
be more complete than his,
occupied by successful men in suits?

We need a prophet. Things must change.
But how?

1982; revised 2006, 2017.

The Aim of Life

"The aim of life is to develop our souls:

"Like the Wanderer—
that Anglo-Saxon pilgrim—
who saw his journey, through life,
as a struggle, to return to a heaven,
that had inexplicably banished him;
sent him out from the warm fireside,
where men huddle against monsters
and inhospitable nature;
secure in the companionship of man,
secure under the patronage
of the warring and feudal lord;

"Like Wordsworth's child,
born in the presence of God's glory—
his vision of eternity
dulled by living in the world—
bitterly regretting
the distance from God, that life brings,
and fighting to live, in such a way,
as to regain God's bright presence
after death."

So we were taught in school.

Religion, philosophy, morality,
the world's literatures—
these were central to our studies;

for they showed us the way to live,
to secure safe passage to heaven at death;
and the trumpets' sound for us on the other side.

Science, technology,
were merely means
to illustrate God's might,
spreading our knowledge of Him.

By reducing the toil of life,
they left more time to study Him.

But now Society has forgotten God,
no longer views, as actual,
immortality of the individual
(for man may soon destroy
the whole human race for ever).

Now come to this pass,
what part can the humanities play?

Technology is all-important.
It can kill us. It can starve us. It can feed us.
It can do almost all that God could do.

Soon it will do anything.

In this world,
only technology
seems relevant.

All the humanities can do is teach us
how to live in a technological world;
how to adjust our values and desires to cope.

A whole study,
whose very ethos teaches its own primacy,
is forced into irrelevance...
subordination to a knowledge
it must believe is secondary.

No wonder we—
trained in the humanities—
are sad, suicidal, frustrated,
aggressive and depressed.

Should we fight against the general current of things?
Or—more difficult—against our common sense?
...insisting— but how argue this? —
that our own pursuits and skills are central?

Or, should we accept
that we—who chose the humanities,
because of our desire to work
on the most important—
are now firmly lodged
in work, which is peripheral;
and have no hope
—at this time of our lives—
to gain sufficient expertise,
studying the new gods
—of technology—
and the morality they insist on:

(cruel gods who require our sacrifice
of loyalty, unselfishness, endurance and love
—qualities, centuries have nurtured—
our sacrifice, also, of our previous choice
of future good over present gratification;
the distant not the immediate goal).

It cannot be that we must bend our skills,
our love of whatsoever things are true,
whatsoever things are pure,
whatsoever things are good and of good report;
our search to make man worthy of God's love
and man's eternal destiny, given by God.

It cannot be, that we must strive, now,
to help man live his life alone;
in harmony only with machines,
that man has made.

Written c. 1982; edited 2006; revised 2007, 2017.

International Intimacies

We meet. We part.
In between
we make acquaintance, become friends,
understand how much we have in common,
how we complement each other;
see what we could do together
if we did not live
across the world...

across cultures too.

But these aren't the problem.

These we transcend easily,
finding common ground:—
music, cultures we admire,
causes we support,
experiences, ideas,
global news we share,
compassionate objects
that have moved us
equally.

We teeter on the edges
of such deep intimacy
that we withdraw;
experience the empty feelings
of incipient depression.

Is it too much to cherish?—
this sudden intimacy of the shared cause,
that our international meetings focused on,
and which we can—no, will—pursue.

But we have other lives.

We return to them. These relationships
descend deep within our daily consciousness.

Some of us will treasure them;
restore them, when we meet again.

Some will be angry or disappointed,
that constant communication
did not continually vibrate across the wires.

The seeds fell on the deepest ground,
began to sprout bright green;

but the field was already occupied.

2009

Cats

Experiment: to stare in the eyes of the black jaguar in the Hong Kong Botanic Gardens.

Was Blake right
when he talked of tigers' eyes as bright?
Was Kipling right,
when he claimed,
no animal can meet the gaze of man,
steadily, unafraid?

Kipling's wolf-child,
Mowgli,
looks up, innocently,
at the big beasts,
making them turn their heads,
uneasy and ashamed.

An adolescent, Mowgli knew his power,
used it deliberately,
to gain a point
in the council of the jungle,
or to deflect brute attack on him,
the weakest of the beasts.

But I have looked in the eyes of big cats too.

They are not bright.

They burn with intelligence
of neither man, nor brute.

They don't slightly turn aside
their heads; but still they will not meet my gaze.
This happens...

The tiger's head directly faces mine.
I place myself before his eyes.
I try to intercept
what consciousness is there,
behind the eyes: in vain.

What does he focus on?

He does not...see
(but feign he does not see) me.
Simply there is something else
on which it seems his gaze alights.
Nor does he see through me.
—I do not think he consciously
decides to cut me (as a social lion might).—

Something else preoccupies his soul.

There is nothing the other side of me,
or in the real distance beyond;
there is nothing substantial there,
on which his darkness rests.

Perhaps his eyes are full of forests—
leaves and dark lianas,
climbing up and round,
and butterflies,
with decisive indecision,
flitting round—
reflected there, from times, when,
as a cub, he gambolled free.

Over the Years: Selected Collected Poems

But if they are,
these past experiences
leave no impression
on his mind.

Of course, tigers have a low IQ!
Not as high as 5 or 10....
Of non-ape beasts, pigs are the most intelligent;
And even they score a mere 18.

This tiger would not comprehend
the insolent defiance of a man.
He could not feel uncomfortable
if a man gazed in his eyes.
For he would not see, not register the event.

Indeed he's forged on Blakean anvil by a hand divine,
set going by the divine clockmaker
to crash and tear and snarl and stink
in a damp darkness, occasionally riven by the light.

Cats are another matter.
Domesticated over time themselves,
they know this domestic creature, man.
They have learnt his desire
for undeserved authority
and pander to it just so far.

They gaze back
when a man stares hard into their eyes;
then turn their look away, after a while.

Man thinks his greatly-loved companion cat
pretends this game is boring.

Really, he thinks,
his cat acknowledges
his own authority
by this veer in gaze.—
Each man thinks himself
the grown Mowgli,
strong and brave.

In fact, domesticated cats
merely indulge their man.

For in their other actions,
cats all show the low opinion
that they hold of him;

behave to him—
not intimately,
as towards other cats—
but treat him as an inanimate thing;
a being of no consequence,
except as a something
to rub against
to satisfy some itch.

Tigers and cats—
caged in a zoo,
or in our homes—
all know how to put us
in our conceptual place!

Hong Kong, [2009?]; revised 2017.

Embodiment

Matta-Rouch Trio (France), concert at Ordino, Andorra, part of the Eleventh Gathering of Bagpipers.

Gravely, with sonorous bold
discords, they reveal
the music
that stained-glass-window saints
and faded fresco angels made
before God, long centuries ago;
the sudden brief sweet
melody equally pleasing
to His ears.

The pace increases—excited,
running away.—God's
foot surely tapped too.

Then the sparkling finale!

The performance achieved,
angels and saints possess
their hearers' souls.

Artist adherents, inspired,
give the heard music
colour and form,
showing us sounds
otherwise silenced by time,
change,
and lack of constancy.

Ordino, August 2009

Choices

A long life has much to say for it;
one must select what to say.
And life itself—however long—is itself
a selection from what might have been done.
You chose, it seems,
service to other men's words and meanings;
in libraries, on a publisher's—then editor's—
desk, as speech-writer and breaker of codes.

And the place where you chose to live—somewhat
predetermined by your place of birth,
Wuhan, Hubei, in China (a missionary's son)—
also, it seems, signposted your life-time's work
(Asia, Asian Studies, mainly),
and excluded—or at least diminished—
other subjects that you might equally
have beamed your search-light on.

We have benefited from these choices;
also from your courtesy, concern
and conscientiousness, and yes,
from your curiosity and cushioning too.

You persisted in teasing-out
other men's meanings. Doubtless
you knew your own meanings too.

Is there anyone left who will unpick
your puzzle for us all to read,
and then, know you better than we did?

2010; revised 2017.

Eden Marriage Registry

Walking towards the Macau Ferry Terminal,
something caught my eye:
"Eden Marriage Registry."

Why did it tug so at my sub-conscious,
call for selective attention
from among the many, richly denotative objects
in this urban—but not urbane—harbour location;
where China steamers have come and gone
for a century and more,
bringing east and west into touch?

"Eden?" The person who chose the name
must surely have heard the phrase,
"Happy as in the Garden of Eden,"
and thought "Eden" a good name for a place,
where that beginning of all happiness—
marriage with the one we love—is formalized.

But what about the apple of desire,
the temptation of the serpent,
the ambition of Eve, the reluctant obedience
of her man, Adam, to her advice?

And the consequences!—
banishment from Eden, and the couple's loss
of previous, immortal status?

Is this really what we want
the happy pair to bear in mind,
as they seal their fate;

Then set out perhaps
for the gambling saloon,
as the best way they can find
to mark the biggest gamble of their lives?

Yes, small knowledge is dangerous.

Increasingly,
cross-culturality gives occasion to demonstrate that fact.

*Seen at Central Ferry Piers, Hong Kong,
5 December 2009; revised 2017.*

I Touched the Wall

I touched the wall, my point of turn-
around, and asked myself,
Will this feel of dappled render
come, in time, to be the feel for me
of all accomplishment?—Let me
experiment...
                    ...use this scientific goal
to support
this daily morning walk;
the other daily delights;
and the self-argument—Walking is working too!—
that we must use,
to persuade ourselves away
from instant access to our world of words
on every awakening,
ensuring I enjoy the other walkers;

who—more knowledgeably, perhaps—
with careful exaggeration,
swing their arms;
but whose shorter legs still mean
they walk more slowly through the park;
some halting
to beat their stomachs for purposes unknown;
some—themselves, seemingly uncertain
of their purpose—who slightly call to mind
Shakespeare's schoolboy,
creeping unwillingly to school;
                        some—aging
and sideways bent—determinèdly circle
the grouped palm-trees and laboriously
raise an arm to greet me, as do
the school night-watchmen, now used to me
and my own cheerful wave of hand to them.

The dogs are another matter. Some know
their purposes are publicly to perform
private acts efficiently, quickly,
and as copiously as possible;
know their companions, slightly embarrassed,
secretly dislike the task of walking them,
making it palatable by texting friends, reading the paper,
and generally, "walking the dog," as little as they can.

But others happily take their humans for a walk,
unleashed illegally; and I hold back
from greeting them, unwilling either to
seduce or be snapped at, to be sniffed too
intimately—among strangers, after all!

But let us continue....

Here is the tiny knot garden,
its sturdy tall shrubs enlivened by delicate flowers.

The China Sea....
A single small boat pulls in its nets,
son helping mother perhaps,
to continue this dying occupation,
until, hakka hat put aside,
she rows to another shore
and he seeks work on land.

More distant, a boat sits, with its four
elongated, jointed, crustacean legs
awaiting its bigger catch.

In the distance, Hong Kong and Kowloon hills
and other heights are seen through a haze that
Turner would have liked to paint. (Another day,
a rising sun turns ones eyes away.)
To the right, absent egrets on a single tree
and close shore line....

—The other day, something
had disturbed them. They had risen up
and now wheeled around; and
it was interesting to see the pattern
of their reattachment to the land;
some quickly crowded the tree; some took
the opportunity to take a break
from the crowd, and stayed relatively long away.
In fact, some took so long I resumed my walk:
No time to observe them further.—

Low tide...
and a little sandy beach, beneath
the rubber tires, broken witches' hat and other
mysteries of modern use; now disused, diseased,
awaiting a small boy or stranded sea-farer,
to provide new use and sense of purpose...

which we all need—objects, birds, dogs, people—
to feel whole, wholesome and free of nothingness.

Discovery Bay, Hong Kong
27 September 2010; revised 2017.

Water

The gardener drew a magic circle of water-drops
around him and her, sitting, reading their papers,
staring at their inner thoughts.

But me he slightly dampened,
sprinkling bag and baggage
with precious drops;
wanting to reach through me to the thirsty plants beyond.

This happened today.

And the message was?

When someone appears
bringing freshness to life,
remove obstructions,
be receptive;
let the drops of novelty—however inconvenient—
touch you. Receive the message,
and grow from its touch!

Hong Kong Park,
2011

Editor's Choice

FROM *FOR THE RECORD*

'For the Record'
    A reminder of the transitory nature of life by referring to old photographs.

'Survival'
    Trees are present now and will survive in the future, despite pollution and other dangers.

'The Creator Commands His Own Creation'
    A memory that stems from a concert given in Hong Kong by a (now late) distinguished conductor of 'classical' music.

'Second Thoughts'
    A comment on the need to retain possessions, despite a wish to abandon them.

'Moon-Shine'
    Comments on the purpose of the Moon and a suggestion that it should make its presence felt more widely.

'Ching Ming Festival'
    The somewhat melancholy thoughts of an ancestor after injuries had been sustained by his family at the 1991 Ching Ming Festival fire that took place in Hong Kong.

'Memories Of School: Admiration'
    References to a school teacher's real opinion of the girls that she had taught.

'An Intense Desire to be Oneself'
    The refusal of a millipede to give way to an attempt by a human to kill it is set against the reluctance of six male hospital patients to obey hospital 'rules.'

FROM *MOVING HOUSE*

'Past Present'
    A commentary on the fragility of life and, in particular, a contrast between past and present.

'Christmas Letters from Afar.'
    Souls from past and present lives are remembered.

'Fortune Teller'
    A granddaughter seeks advice from a fortune teller.

'Scene in the Street'
    Advice is taken after losing a pair of gloves.

'Progressive Movement'
    Discoveries were made when cycling in New Zealand.

'Conferees'
    Freedom! The debaters were let loose for lunch.

'(Em-) Brace (-Let)'
    The unhappy boy. A sad tale.

'Change with Constancy'
    An assurance came from the goddess.

'A Pure Devotion'
    The gods were benevolent on this occasion.

'What I Wanted to Say'
    Thoughts from a daughter at a father's death-bed.

FROM *SIGHTINGS*

'Super-ego'
    A successful search.

'Take up your Bed and Walk!'
    The palsy was defeated.

'Politically Correct?'
    Hypocrisy and Idealism are explained.

'Parish Priest'
    The devoted priest.

'Walking Stick'
    A stick accompanied Father.

'Transit Lounge'
    Thoughts at an airport when waiting for a flight. A way of passing the time.

'White Flags'
    Fresh flags were erected near the graves.

'Fragile Symbols'
    Meanings for the symbols.

'Her Choice'
    The lady in white. She had/has an unusual taste in garments.

'Aperçus'
    A walk around the Peak.

'The Watcher Watched'
    The copy cats.

FROM *CHINA SUITE*

'Wish you were here in Hong Kong'
    We have Flowers, Animals, Birds, Streams, Snakes, Pylons, Engines, Music, Dogs, Hills and much, much more.

'Seen in Shanghai'
    Mother and handicapped son are making the best of it.

'Gangways'
    Some thoughts on the ferry bound for Discovery Bay.

'Fisherwoman II: She loved the Sea.'
    Questions about funerals when at sea. There are pluses and minuses.

'Applause, or A Simply Ambiguous Life.'
    What was left out of her speech? Was it titillating?

'Communicable Smile'
    You have to understand the smile when it comes as a surprise.

'The Flute-Player: Sweet and Low.'
    His well-played tune has an impact on everyone who hears it.

'Penates'
    A reminder can be useful. Sometimes it may be essential. So follow the journalist's advice and always take your 'Penates.'

'Word-diggers'
    The digging is for words, sometimes the writer's gold. Like all gold, it can be difficult to find.

'Caring Professionals:'
   Perhaps they mean well, but their record is less than perfect, as the professionals might admit.

'Pumpkin Man.'
   The last published poem in the collection. A sad reference to a handicapped beggar, but it does seem that he has a home of sorts to go to.

FROM *PERCEPTIONS*

'Added Value'
   What should we value most? That is the question. An answer is given,

'Change, Please'
   The suggestion is that the European's culture should, somehow, be changed to be of benefit to everyone.

'The Aim of Life'
   The aim of life is to develop our souls. Still religion, philosophy, morality, literature. But science or technology?

'International Intimacies'
   We know they are transitory but sometimes we hope for more. It is, after all, a two-way street and sometimes it is necessary to cross to the other side.

'Cats'
   Do they respect us as we respect them? But do we <u>really</u> respect them? Are we merely affected by their proud demeanour?

'Embodiment'
   The musicians play and reach beyond themselves. Their dulcet sounds reach far into the Andorran night and into the expectant hills.

'Choices'
>This has a place in an anthology describing the lives of adventurous men. As written, we have benefited from your actions and your thoughts.

'Eden Marriage Registry'
>Eden. On the way to Macau for an enquiry, or a marriage But also a politician and Prime Minister, with foreign adventures foiled, perhaps contemplating the Way of the World and its foibles.

'I Touched the Wall'
>A simple, everyday act. Not Shakespeare's Wall, but walking with a purpose and waiting for the signal to turn. Passing other walkers, friendly and unfriendly dogs, boats, birds, gardens and hills. Then back to the start.

'Water'
>More than just drops and wetness. There is a message to learn.

Verner Bickley

VERNER BICKLEY is the Editor of *Poems to Enjoy*, Books 1 to 5, inclusive, first published in London by the University of London Press, 1960. A second, selected, edition was published in Hong Kong by Hong Kong Educational Publishing Co. with cassette tapes of readings of the poems, and a third edition, also in Hong Kong, by Proverse Hong Kong, with the original poems restored and new digitised recordings on CDs of all poems in each of the five books.

Message from Dumitru M. Ion

Driven by curiosity as a poet but also by responsibility as the president of, "The International Festival Curtea de Argeş Poetry Nights," in Romania (There have been twenty editions, attended in total by over fifteen hundred guests from about a hundred countries), I read and translate the lyrics of hundreds of poets.

That's how I discovered the exceptional poet Gillian Bickley from Hong Kong.

What firstly drew my attention was the savant level of her poetry; the science of balancing the rational with the sentiment.

Each of her poems is sometimes a small novel, an essay or at other times a lyrical sublimate. Her poems are remembrances: from the past (an ancient past, a medieval past, and so on), from her own past or a possible reader's past.

The way of shaping her poetry especially fascinates the professional reader. Because, of course, a professional poet (as Gillian Bickley is) will always need a professional reader.

Dumitru M. Ion
Romania
Member of the Arts and Sciences Academy
    in R. Macedonia, etc.

Notes

[1] Inspired by the following sentences in an assignment on Laurie Lee's *Cider with Rosie*, written by Rita Lee Po Yu, Hong Kong Baptist University student of Discursive Prose (ENG 1170), 2003/2004, taught by this writer: "We miss the past because we came from there. As we get older, we have more memories and are even more reluctant to change."

[2] Miss Lesley Hart, a friend of the writer and a public librarian, very kindly researched this lady for the writer, sometime after this poem was first published. One of the pieces of information she kindly sent shows a photograph with the following caption: "Elsie Wood. For many years a familiar and imposing figure as she glided around town, all in white, including her parasol and deathly make-up, and looking neither to left nor right. Her regal perambulations earned her various nicknames such as 'The Woman in White', 'The Queen of Sheba', and 'Queen Mary'. Popular legend told of her having been jilted into the strangeness of her ways." The accompanying photograph, however, dated 10 November 1957, shows Miss Wood wearing mainly black and the caption further comments, "When this photograph was taken (by pure chance) as she waited for a bus near Shrub Hill station, she had more or less forsaken white in favour of black."
See also:
http://www.worcesternews.co.uk/news/7647606.Colleague_s_recollections_of_Worcester_s_Lady_in_White/

[3] Cf. "Auguste", the name of the type of circus clown who has his face painted white.

[4] All architectural and place references are to the City of Worcester, in the English Midlands. The Star, The Angel and The Crown are all establishments serving alcoholic liquor, as well as providing rooms in which to stay.

[5] Here used as a euphemism for "alcoholic liquor".
[6] "Grey Friars" is a name given to the Franciscans, or Friars Minor, an order founded by St Francis of Assisi. Presumably, "Grey Friars", an old building in the centre of modern Worcester city, was once a Franciscan friary, or had some other relationship to the Franciscans. (The present building dates from c1480. The Dissolution of the Monasteries under King Henry VIII took place in 1536.)
[7] "The Shambles" is a shopping area in Worcester city, previously the area where butchers carried out their business.
[8] Hops (from which beer is made) are a traditional Worcestershire crop.
[9] Meetings of The Society of Friends (members are also called "Quakers") have no set "service" as many other Christian groups have. Members sit in silence and any, who feel inspired to contribute some thoughts, speak up spontaneously. The group opposes war and violence.
[10] Cavaliers and Roundheads wore different styles of clothes, had different hair-styles, spoke differently and worshipped God differently.
[11] Worcester came to be referred to in this way after the two English Civil Wars, because of its loyalty to both Charles I (king, 1625-1649 (when he was executed)) and his son, Charles II (crowned, defeated and fled to France in 1651; restored as king, 1660-1685). Worcester city was first in declaring support for King Charles I and the last to surrender to Cromwell in 1646. The final battle of the second civil war was the Battle of Worcester, 1651, when Charles II was finally defeated.
[12] Ordinary people might go on a tour. A monarch made a "progress" through his or her realm.

ABOUT PROVERSE HONG KONG

Proverse Hong Kong is based in Hong Kong with expanding long-term regional and international connections.

Proverse has published novels, novellas, short-story collections, fictionalized autobiography, non-fiction (including autobiography, biography, Hong Kong educational and legal history, memoirs, travel narratives, sport), poetry and single-author poetry collections, academic and supplementary educational books, as well as children's and teens / young adult books. Other interests include diaries, and academic works in the humanities, social sciences, cultural studies, linguistics and education.

Some Proverse books have accompanying audio texts. Some are translated into Chinese.

Proverse welcomes authors who have a story to tell, wisdom, perceptions or information to convey, a person they want to memorialize, a neglect they want to remedy, a record they want to correct, a strong interest that they want to share, skills they want to teach, and who consciously seek to make a contribution to society in an informative, interesting and well-written way. Proverse works with texts by non-native-speaker writers of English as well as by native English-speaking writers.

The name, "Proverse", combines the words "prose" and "verse" and is pronounced accordingly.

THE INTERNATIONAL PROVERSE PRIZE

The Proverse Prize, an annual international competition for an unpublished book-length work of fiction, non-fiction, or poetry, was established in January 2008. Unusually for a competition of this nature, it is open to all who are at least eighteen on the date they sign the entry form and without restriction of nationality, residence or citizenship, including new, emerging and established writers.

The objectives of the Proverse Prize are: to encourage excellence and / or excellence and usefulness in publishable written work in the English Language, which can, in varying degrees, "delight and instruct." Entries are invited from anywhere in the world. Long-listed writers to date include writers born or resident in Andorra, Australia, Canada, Germany, Hong Kong, New Zealand, Nigeria, Singapore, Taiwan, The Bahamas, the PRC, the United Arab Emirates, the United Kingdom, the USA.

Summary Terms and Conditions
(for indication only & subject to revision)
The information below is for guidance only. Please refer to the year-specific Proverse Prize Entry Form & Terms & Conditions, which are uploaded, no later than 14 April each year, onto the Proverse Hong Kong website: <www.proversepublishing.com>.

The free Proverse e-Newsletter includes ongoing information about the Proverse Prize. To be put on the eNewsletter mailing-list, please email: info@proversepublishing.com with your request.

The Prize
1) Publication by Proverse Hong Kong, with
2) Cash prize of HKD10,000 (HKD7.80 = approx. US$1.00)

Supplementary publication grants may be made to selected other entrants for publication by Proverse Hong Kong.

Depending on the quality of the work in any year, the prize may be shared by at most two entrants or withheld, as recommended by the judges.

In 2017, the entry fee is: HKD320.00 OR GBP35.00.

Writers are eligible, who are at least eighteen on the date they sign The Proverse Prize entry documents. There is no nationality or residence restriction.

Each submitted work must be an unpublished publishable single-author work of non-fiction, fiction or poetry, the original work of the entrant, and submitted in the English language. School textbooks and plays are ineligible.

Unpublished first translations into English (including those already published in the writer's mother tongue) submitted by the author are welcome. The submitted work will not be judged as a translation but as an original work.

Extent of the Manuscript: within the range of what is usual for the genre of the work submitted. However, it is advisable that novellas be in the range 30,000 to 45,000 words); other fiction (e.g. novels, short-story collections) and non-fiction (e.g. autobiographies, biographies, diaries, letters, memoirs, essay collections, etc.) should be in the range, 75,000 to 100,000 words. Poetry / poetry collections should be in the range, 5,000 to 25,000 words. Other word-counts and mixed-genre submissions are not ruled out.

Writers may choose, if they wish, to obtain the services of an Editor in presenting their work, and should acknowledge this help and the nature and extent of this help in the Entry Form.

KEY DATES FOR THE PROVERSE PRIZE IN ANY YEAR
(subject to confirmation and/or change)

Entry period	[No later than] 14 April to 14 June of the year of entry
Announcement of Semi-finalists (if made)	Usually July-September of the year of entry
Announcement of Finalists	Usually October-December of the year of entry
Announcement of winner/ max two winners (sharing the cash prize)	December of the year of entry to April of the year that follows the year of entry
Cash Award Made	At the same time as publication of the work(s) adjudged the winner(s) of the Proverse Prize
Publication of winning work(s)	In or after November of the year that follows the year of entry

Over the Years: Selected Collected Poems

THE INTERNATIONAL PROVERSE POETRY PRIZE
(SINGLE POEMS)

An annual international Proverse Poetry Prize (for single poems) was established in 2016. The international Proverse Poetry Prize is open to all who are at least eighteen years old whatever their residence, nationality or citizenship, including new, emerging and established writers.

Single poems, submitted in English, are invited on (a) <u>any subject or theme, chosen by the writer</u> OR (b) <u>on a subject or theme selected by the organizers each year</u>.

Poems may be in any form, style or genre. Each poem should be no more than 30 lines, not counting the title or blank lines.

Entries should previously be unpublished in any way (except in the case of unpublished translations into English of the entrant's own work already published in another language, providing the entrant holds the copyright).

In 2016, cash prizes were offered as follows:
1st prize; USD100.00; 2nd prize: USD45.00;
3rd prizes (up to four winners): USD20.00.

KEY DATES FOR THE PROVERSE POETRY PRIZE IN 2017
(subject to confirmation and/or change)

Receipt of entered work, entry forms and entry fees	7 May to 30 June of the year of entry
Announcement of Winners	April, or earlier, of the year following the year of entry
Cash Awards Made	At the same time as publication of the winning poems (whether in the Proverse newsletter or website, or in an anthology)
Publication of an anthology of winning and other selected entries	Contingent on the quality of entries in any year

The information above is for guidance only.
More information, updated from time to time, is available from the Proverse website: proversepublishing.com

SOME POETRY AND POETRY COLLECTIONS
Published by Proverse Hong Kong

Astra and Sebastian, by L.W. Illsley. 2011.
Bliss of Bewilderment, by Birgit Bunzel Linder.
Chasing light, by Patricia Glinton Meicholas. 2013.
China suite and other poems, by Gillian Bickley. 2009.
For the record and other poems of Hong Kong,
 by Gillian Bickley. 2003.
Frida Kahlo's Cry and Other Poems,
 by Laura Solomon. 2015.
Home, away, elsewhere, by Vaughan Rapatahana. 2011.
Immortelle and bhandaaraa poems,
 by Lelawattee Manoo-Rahming. 2011.
In vitro, by Laura Solomon. 2nd ed. 2014.
Irreverent Poems for Pretentious People,
 by Henrik Hoeg. 2016.
*Mingled Voices: The International Proverse Poetry Prize
 Anthology 2016.* 2017.
Moving house and other poems from Hong Kong,
 by Gillian Bickley. 2005.
Of Leaves & Ashes, by Patty Ho. 2016.
Of symbols misused, by Mary-Jane Newton. 2011.
Painting the borrowed house: poems,
 by Kate Rogers. 2008.
Perceptions, by Gillian Bickley. 2012.
Rain on the pacific coast, by Elbert Siu Ping Lee. 2013.
refrain, by Jason S. Polley. 2010.
Shadow play, by James Norcliffe. 2012.
Shadows in Deferment, by Birgit Bunzel Linder. 2013.
Shifting Sands, by Deepa Vanjani. 2016.
*Sightings: a collection of poetry, with an essay, 'communicating
 poems'*, by Gillian Bickley. 2007.
Smoked pearl: poems of Hong Kong and beyond,
 by Akin Jeje (Akinsola Olufemi Jeje). 2010.
The Layers Between (Essays and Poems),
 by Celia Claase. 2015.
Unlocking, by Mary-Jane Newton. March 2014.
Wonder, lust & itchy feet, by Sally Dellow. 2011.

FIND OUT MORE ABOUT OUR AUTHORS, BOOKS, EVENTS AND LITERARY PRIZES

Visit our website:
http://www.proversepublishing.com

Visit our distributor's website: <www.chineseupress.com>

Follow us on Twitter
Follow news and conversation: twitter.com/Proversebooks>
OR
Copy and paste the following to your browser window and follow the instructions:
https://twitter.com/#!/ProverseBooks
"Like" us on www.facebook.com/ProversePress

Request our free E-Newsletter
Send your request to info@proversepublishing.com.

Availability
Most titles are available in Hong Kong and world-wide from our Hong Kong based Distributor,
The Chinese University of Hong Kong Press,
The Chinese University of Hong Kong, Shatin, NT,
Hong Kong SAR, China.
Email: cup-bus@cuhk.edu.hk
Website: <www.chineseupress.com>.
All titles are available from Proverse Hong Kong
http://www.proversepublishing.com
and the Proverse Hong Kong UK-based Distributor.

We have **stock-holding retailers** in Hong Kong,
Singapore (Select Books),
Canada (Elizabeth Campbell Books),
Andorra (Llibreria La Puça, La Llibreria).
Orders can be made from bookshops in the UK and elsewhere.

Ebooks
Most of our titles are available also as Ebooks.

www.ingramcontent.com/pod-product-compliance
Lightning Source LLC
Chambersburg PA
CBHW071701170426
43195CB00039B/2444